W O R K B O O K

Family
TIES

RESTORING UNITY IN THE
AFRICAN AMERICAN FAMILY

WRITTEN BY
REV. CHERYL P. CLEMETSON, PH.D.
EVANGELINE CAREY

EDITED BY
KATHRYN HALL

UMI (Urban Ministries, Inc.)
Chicago, Illinois

TABLE OF CONTENTS

PREFACE

The *Family Ties: Restoring Unity in the African American Family Workbook* for students is to be used in conjunction with the book, *Family Ties: Restoring Unity in the African American Family*, written by Colleen Birchett, Ph.D. This compelling book contains vignettes from a collection of Bible families, paired with vignettes from African American family life. Each chapter is devoted to a different biblical principle and begins with a story about contemporary African American families. It then presents background information on the historical context of the biblical family and offers guidance to draw insights for modern applications. In so doing, the book provides the opportunity to study and reflect upon the stories and to draw on the wisdom of these timeless principles to reunite and reinvigorate the family unit.

This *Family Ties: Restoring Unity in the African American Family Workbook* for students contains a corresponding series of questions that allow the reader to explore how the biblical passages and the contemporary stories relate to the state of many African American families today. It is designed to help the reader to connect the biblical principles and real life situations found in the chapters of the book and apply them to the circumstances and challenges that confront the family of God and their respective biological families as well. This workbook will attempt to assist individuals who engage themselves with responding to the Life Application Questions, the Bible Application Exercises, and the Personal Application activities with understanding the futility of trying to achieve unity and/or strength in the nuclear or in the extended family without a proper spiritual foundation. It will reinforce and reiterate the vital need to include God, our heavenly Father, in the quest to strengthen and restore the African American family to unity in Christ Jesus.

The *Family Ties: Restoring Unity in the African American Family Workbook* questions can be beneficial as take-home assignments as well as in daily devotions. The *Family Ties: Restoring Unity in the African American Family* adult study course, consisting of the student textbook, leader's guide, and this workbook can be used in a variety of Christian Education settings, including: family based or small group studies, weekday Bible studies, church-wide retreats, church school electives, book clubs, Vacation Bible School courses, and Christian Education Congresses.

STARTING OVER VS. REMAINING THE SAME

John 3:1-16; John 7:37-52; 19:37-42

"In reply Jesus declared, "I tell you the truth, no one can see the kingdom of God unless he is born again." (John 3:3, NIV).

Lesson Focus: God's Family Begins—Jesus taught Nicodemus that to become a member of the family of God, he must be born again of the Spirit of God. This is the ultimate life-transforming message for us, as well as the key to receiving salvation through Jesus Christ. Being born again puts us in a right relationship with God. It also brings about a new opportunity to get our relationships with other people in order—our family members, neighbors, and all people within our communities and beyond.

Word and Phrases You Should Know
In preparation for the lesson, familiarize yourself with the following definitions:
- **Grapevine**—Passing on news about church, family, work, etc., by word of mouth
- **Giving the heart to Jesus**—Asking God for forgiveness; believing on the Lord Jesus Christ, the One who paid our sin-penalty; and calling on God for salvation
- **Exacerbate**—To add negativity to a problem or situation
- **Made in the image of God**—Christ-likeness; patterned after Him
- **Had a little talk with Jesus**—Having a conversation with Jesus; talking to Him in prayer
- **Take off the old self and enter a new life**—Shedding the past sinful life and walking in the newness that Christ gives through His Holy Spirit

LIFE APPLICATION DISCUSSION QUESTIONS
State your own personal views in answering the following questions.

1. When did you decide to follow Jesus? Include in your explanation any details that bring this life-transforming event to life.

_____

_____

_____

2. How comfortable do you feel witnessing to others about Christ? Are there any barriers that you experience that keep you from witnessing for Christ?

_____

_____

_____

3. How would you rate or describe your honesty with Christ and with yourself about who you are and your Christian walk.

_____

_____

_____

4. In your family, who is the person considered to be the "religious one" and/or the person you seek godly counsel from? If this person is not a "born-again" believer, why do you trust his or her advice? What can you learn from him or her and how can you better share the Good News of Jesus Christ with this person?

_____

_____

_____

BIBLE APPLICATION EXERCISES

1. Being Born into the Family of God

Themes of anticipation, holding on to the past, uncertainty, and a new beginning are some of the themes that are found in the chapter 1 introductory story and the section titled, "A Closer Look at Nicodemus." In the Scripture text, Jesus addresses how we must be born again. However, life brings about challenges and concerns when we have to make changes in our lives that will bring us closer to God. But the good news is that Jesus has given each of us a second chance.

Read the verses below and describe how each passage related to being born into the family of God. (Answers will vary.)

a. John 1:12-13

_____

_____

_____

b. John 3:3-5

_____

_____

_____

c. John 3:16

_____

_____

_____

Personal Application

State your views about the following questions:

1. How can the past hold us back from a new beginning? Give examples.

_____

_____

_____

2. Give two or three reasons why you think people are hesitant to publicly profess their faith in Jesus so that others will come to know Him.

_____

_____

_____

3. Why are Christians selective in what they publicly protest as injustice over social issues? Remembering that Jesus challenged injustice by all, what social policies do you believe Christians should stand up against and speak out on?

_____

_____

_____

2. Nicodemus—A Second Chance

   a. Take some time to think about how Jesus gave Nicodemus a second chance. Read the following biblical stories and share your insights on what is the second chance that is being offered and why you think another chance was given.

   1) Adam and Eve (Genesis 3:6–7, 21–23)

_____

_____

   2) Jairus's Daughter (Luke 8:49–56)

_____

_____

   3) Paul's Conversion (Acts 9:1–6)

_____

_____

b. After reading John 3:1-16, how does knowing Jesus in your life and in the lives of people in your family help to give your family a second chance?

_____

_____

c. Share with others an opportunity in which you can describe how the family was given a second chance or a new beginning.

_____

_____

_____

Personal Application

1. Think of a Scripture or Bible Story that describes how Jesus has given you a second chance. Then give the Scripture reference _____.

_____

_____

_____

2. Who are the biblical characters that you most identify with as having a new beginning, a second chance?

_____

_____

_____

3. Do you see your family as growing closer together and stronger? Describe why or why not? What will need to happen for the family to either begin again or build on the foundation that you already have?

_____

_____

_____

3. Being a Part of the Solution

a. Reflect on ways that you can help the Nicodemus in your life accept being born again. Role-play with someone else the characters of Jesus and Nicodemus to help you feel comfortable sharing your faith story, which will witness to that person's needs rather than where you think they should be. Write down a few opening sentences to help you focus on what you may say and be prepared to report on your experience as you practiced.

_____

_____

_____

b. Compile a list of Scriptures that will lead a person to accept Jesus Christ as their personal Savior, that can also be used in conjunction with the role-play above.

_____

_____

_____

c. Discuss some of the hindrances that prevent people from witnessing to others about Christ. Name some ways these challenges can be overcome.

_____

_____

_____

Personal Application

1. Jesus did not condemn Nicodemus for coming to Him in the night. Jesus knew Nicodemus and knows our needs as well. Therefore, He will have patience and work with us if we want to act as undercover Christians. Jesus is the Light and He knows how to share His light with us. Ask God to show you how to effectively witness and minister to others and to yourself about the love and light of Jesus Christ.

2. Think of three to five family members that you believe need to know more about the light of Jesus Christ and His love. List them below. Spend time talking with them or ministering to them in such a way that the light of Jesus will come shining through you to them. Sometimes we do not always have to preach a sermon to show people Jesus. Our actions often do speak louder than our words.

_____   _____

_____   _____

_____

The Family Ties Commitment Activity

Being born of the Spirit is the greatest new beginning we will ever know. As we learn more about ourselves and experience life, what are some of the areas you would like to change in your family?

a. Family Issues/Concern

_____

_____

b. Estranged Siblings/Others

_____

_____

c. Financial Burdens

_____

_____

d. Children (all ages)

_____

_____

e. Illness

_____

_____

f. Employment

_____

_____

g. Unsaved

_____

_____

h. Anger Management

_____

_____

i. Other

_____

_____

Write a song, prayer, or draw a picture that gives hope to how the Lord can work in your family for a positive and healthy change.

_____

_____

_____

_____

Amen.

COOPERATING VS. COMPETING

Genesis 27:34-35, 41; 33:1-4, 8-11

"For if you forgive men when they sin against you, your heavenly Father will also forgive you"
(Matthew 6:14, NIV).

Lesson Focus: God's Family Forgives—When we think we deserve particular blessings or gifts, we can sometimes manipulate or take extreme measures to make it happen. The story of Jacob and Esau highlights how humans sometimes do not mind doing underhanded things to accomplish our goals. With the help of his mother, Rebecca, Jacob tricked his father into giving him the blessing for a first-born male child. Jacob is later tricked by his uncle Laban into marrying the oldest daughter Leah, instead of the woman he loved, the youngest daughter, Rachel. In the interest of bringing about the outcome they desired, both Rebecca and Laban practiced deception and involved their children in schemes to get their way. Unfortunately, the deceptive plots created pain and sorrow for the children in many ways. Yet, God worked in the midst of the deception and distress to bless the children of Israel and to continue setting the scene for the birth of Christ. The bloodline of Jesus is traced through Jacob and Rachel. We are reminded that God is still in control and does not stop being God because we may choose to be disobedient and deceitful to God or others.

Words and Phrases You Should Know
In preparation for the lesson, familiarize yourself with the following definitions:
- Resiliency factors—Consistent strengths of African American families: strong achievement orientation; strong work orientation; flexibility of family roles; strong kinship bonds; and a strong religious orientation (Robert Hill)
- Retreat-ism—An escape from the pressure or demands of society; a withdrawal from social life by rejecting morals
- Ghosts of the past—Issues and problems that haven't been resolved in a society or one's personal life (i.e., abuse, institutionalized racism)
- Counter culture—A different way of life or norms from that established by the majority or governing power (i.e., Rosa Parks and others protesting segregated bus rides)

LIFE APPLICATION DISCUSSION QUESTIONS
State your own personal views in answering the following questions.

1. What can happen when a parent(s) or loved one shows more love or favoritism to one child over another?

_____

_____

_____

2. Name a time in your life when you realized you were treated better or given special treatment over others, even if it was hurtful to someone else. How do you respond when someone else receives favor when you thought you should have received it?

_____

_____

_____

3. Is manipulation of other people always bad? Can it ever be considered good? Find Scriptures to support your answers.

_____

_____

_____

4. Do you ever see or participate in manipulative activities at church, on your job, or in your family? If so, are you praying to ask God to change the situation?

_____

_____

_____

BIBLE APPLICATION EXERCISES

1. Letting Go of the Past

Many Christians join non-Christians in holding grudges against others. Often, we do not want to forgive ourselves. We must realize that holding on to the past is painful and more harmful to us than to others. We forget that Matthew 6:15 declares to us, "But if you do not forgive men their sins, your Father will not forget your sins."

Read the following Scriptures and write your response to how this applies to your life personally and to Christians collectively.

   a. John 5:1-6

   _____

   _____

   b. John 5:7

   _____

   _____

   c. 1 Kings 19:1-2

   _____

   _____

d. 1 Kings 19:3-5

_____

_____

_____

Personal Application

1. Reflect on the relationships in your family where cooperation and competition have been healthy, and times where a lack of cooperation and competition has brought about unhealthy results. Pray about the situation and meditate on James 1:5-6. Then write about how these relationships have affected the family. Finally, write out the guidance that the Holy Spirit will offer you as a solution.

_____

_____

_____

2. How do you handle conflict and disagreements with others who do not like you personally or who may not like your approach to a situation?

_____

_____

_____

3. Respond to the following statement: Having Jesus in my life helps our family to deal with issues and concerns in the following ways:

_____

_____

_____

2. Bait and Switch Routine

There are times when we think that our way is better or helpful to the Lord's way. We find in our story of Jacob and Esau how people can create unnecessary stress and strain in their lives and in the lives of others by taking matters into their own hands. Read Genesis 29:14-29. Answer the following statements based on the biblical account. (Your teacher may share with you some background information about the marriage traditions and culture of that time.)

a. Why do you think Jacob did not realize that Leah was not Rachel?

_____

_____

_____

b. Do you think that an individual's outward appearance affects the judgment of others about the person?

_____

_____

_____

c. Does the text say that Jacob chose Rachel over Leah because of her looks? What are the reasons you find that Rachel was Jacob's preference and not Leah?

_____

_____

_____

d. Are having good looks important in our society at large and in the church? Why or why not?

_____

_____

_____

e. What is your reaction to Laban's behavior toward his daughters and Jacob? What can happen when deceitful behavior runs in a family?

_____

_____

_____

f. Where do you see the presence of God in this story?

_____

_____

_____

Personal Application

Growing up in our respective families, we learn ways to negotiate and navigate through various experiences. Leah, Rachel, and Jacob were encouraged through their parents' choices to lie, hurt others, and allow their frustration or greed to get the better of them. Today, if our families keep practicing unhealthy choices for showing love, comfort, pursuing dreams, raising children, work ethics, education, and so on, how can we work to make healthy choices and decisions? Take time to pray and reflect on your answer to this question.

Read the following Scriptures and apply them to determine what God expects of us and how our actions reflect on those who are in our respective families and in our daily lives. Write your summary below.

a. Psalm 1

_____

_____
_____

b. Psalm 30

_____
_____
_____

c. 1 Corinthians 13

_____
_____
_____

3. Being a Part of the Solution

Some families seem to have more drama and problems than others. Whatever problems or concerns that are in your family or in the church that you are attending, focus new energy into building a healthy family environment.

a. For those you encounter who may be struggling with forgiving family members for past offenses, find three examples in the Bible where forgiveness was necessary in order for the characters involved to move into God's will and receive their blessings. Identify the related Scripture passages below and write out a plan to share these stories with someone in need of God's help to forgive others.

1) _____

2) _____

3) _____

b. Write three tangible ways that you can foster a healthier environment with Jesus at the center of the family.

1) _____

2) _____

3) _____

c. Prayer is always the foundation to discernment, action, and courage to step out on faith. Make a list of people in your family that need your prayers and forgiveness and who also need God's intervention in their lives.

1) _____

2) _____

3) _____

4) _____

5) _____

d. What factors do you think led Esau to forgive his brother Jacob when they reunited several years later? Describe some thoughts Esau may have considered during the time leading up to their reunion.

_____

_____

_____

Personal Application
Consider whether you have ever manipulated someone or a situation? Using your 20/20 hindsight vision, if you had another chance, would you act again in the same way or not?

_____

_____

_____

The Family Ties Commitment Activity
During your next family gathering, ask everyone to recommit their lives to Christ or continue building upon their present relationship with Christ. You may want to also ask everyone to write down a thought or feeling that they need to release about a family member. Then they are to ask God to help them work through and release the thought or feeling. Next, each person is to tear up their paper and throw it away in the "Old Life" trash can. Each person then lifts their hands upward toward God to symbolically receive a fresh start. Finally, everyone brings their hands down in a praying position.

Write a family prayer that centers on letting go and allowing God to work in and through you for a new beginning.

_____

_____

_____

_____

_____

Amen.

"SHARING" VS. "DUMPING"

Ruth 1:8-18; 4:13-16

"Dear friends, let us love one another, for love comes from God. Everyone who loves has been born of God and knows God" (1 John 4:7, NIV).

Lesson Focus: God's Family Loves—God's plan to send man a Savior demonstrated the magnitude of God's love. The relationship between Ruth and Naomi also reflected a love and sharing that was pleasing in God's sight. Instead of abandoning her mother-in-law during a time of intense struggle, Ruth showed a deep sense of loyalty toward Naomi and the power of God's love came forth. Because of Ruth's display of love and courage, God rewarded this young woman's faithfulness as she eventually became instrumental in the birth line of our Savior Jesus Christ.

Words and Phrases You Should Know
In preparation for the lesson, familiarize yourself with the following definitions:
- **Kinship care**—Providing for the parental needs of children within the family
- **Mispaha-Clan**—Family and extended family
- **Goel-Family**—Protector/avenger in relationship to the family, land, debt, slavery, etc.

LIFE APPLICATION DISCUSSION QUESTIONS

State your own personal views in answering the following questions.

1. Is the church a place where you believe a strong sense of loyalty is displayed between the church members?

_____

_____

_____

2. Are people born with qualities such as integrity, honesty, and faithfulness, or are these characteristics learned behaviors? Why do you think these traits are necessary?

_____

_____

_____

3. If Ruth had not followed her heart and stayed close to Naomi, she would have missed a great opportunity. In what ways do people today often miss their blessings?

_____

_____

_____

4. Consider ways that Ruth and Naomi's experience is similar to your own family's experiences. Give comparisons and contrasts. Determine what you have learned from the biblical story that could provide help for your family.

_____

_____

_____

BIBLE APPLICATION EXERCISES

1. A Closer Look

When we read the introductory story of chapter 3, we journey with the heart of a family that has endured financial strife, racial injustice, and separation. We also see how this family was able to respond in crisis and in joy. The Bible presents us with many stories of persons who have been abandoned, rejected, reunited, and loved in their times of despair. Read the following Scriptures and write how you see Jesus and the movement of God expressing love and mercy to those in need.

a. Woman with possessed daughter (Mark 7:25-30)

_____

_____

b. Elijah in the cave (1 Kings 19:9)

_____

_____

c. Moses and the Red Sea (Exodus 14:15-21)

_____

_____

d. The woman caught in adultery (John 8:1-11)

_____

_____

Personal Application

1. What are some ways that Jesus responds to you when feelings of despair, rejection, and loss are heavy on your mind?

_____

_____

_____

2. What are ways that you help lift someone else's spirit and heart when they are feeling unloved or need hope for the future?

_____

_____

_____

2. Sharing and Dumping

Read the following Scriptures and highlight any similarities that you see between your family and the families in the Bible. Write about how the love of Christ has helped to bring a spirit of sharing within the family. Also note any similarities between African American families today and the biblical families, where there might have been tendencies to share love or to dump blame on others. Answers will vary to the following:

    a. Genesis 38:13-19 (Tamar's rejection and revenge)

_____

_____

_____

    b. Genesis 4:8-9 (Cain and Abel—the jealousy and murder)

_____

_____

_____

    c. Matthew 8:14-17 (Peter and his sick mother-in-law)

_____

_____

_____

Personal Application

1. Having trust in someone that you believe offers strength and hope are important keys to helping us make it through dark and uncertain moments in our lives. Janet, the young lady in the introductory story, and Ruth in the Scripture passage both clung to persons they believed would offer them a chance at life. When times are tough for you, who do you cling to and why? List examples of how Jesus was the one for you to cling to in your stormy times.

_____

_____

_____

2. Write three Scriptures from the book of Psalms that give you comfort and trust in the Lord. After writing each of the verses, circle or highlight key word(s) that express a feeling or thought you have about the Lord during your times of weakness.

a. _____

_____

_____

b. _____

_____

_____

c. _____

_____

_____

3. Write three Scriptures from the Gospel of John or Philippians that provide comfort and trust in the Lord. After each of the verses, circle or highlight key word(s) that express a feeling or thought you have about the Lord during your times of weakness.

a. _____

_____

_____

b. _____

_____

_____

c. _____

_____

_____

3. Being a Part of the Solution

We are sometimes tempted to share our ideas and opinions about other people's problems and business. To actively help another family, when was the last time that you personally worked in a ministry other than the Christmas toy drive or the distribution of Thanksgiving food baskets? Pray about where God would want you to serve, and then start serving. If you have a hard time selecting a place or finding the time, choose one Sunday a month to help seniors with their transportation needs, give cards anonymously to those who need a smile, help a parent with childcare needs, volunteer to work in the church office, or stay after church and pick up the programs that are left in the pews and other places.

a. Take a moment to say:

I/we thank you Lord for giving me/us the ability, the strength, and the skill to help someone else. I/we thank you Lord for allowing me/us to be a blessing to someone else and build your Kingdom here on Earth. My commitment is to _____ (activity) by _____. (date)

b. Compare the relationship between Naomi and Ruth with persons that you know and relationships in your personal life.

_____

_____

_____

c. Have you ever reached out to help someone when you were not in a position to care for someone else? Share the experience.

_____

_____

_____

Personal Application

Write a prayer, song, poem, or draw a picture that best illustrates your willingness to care for someone. If you are at a point in your life that you need to take better care of yourself, then first create a prayer, song, poem, or picture that depicts what you need to do for yourself. Then show what you will do for someone else as well.

_____

_____

_____

Family Ties Commitment Activity

God wants families to be healed of their hurts and differences. Show God how serious you are about being a child of God and your desire to please Him. If there is someone you have not spoken to, or held a grudge against, or someone you know that needs help, it is time to do something tangible to make a difference in their lives. Make a commitment to God today that you are ready to do your part in setting things right with your loved ones.

Maybe at your next family reunion or gathering you can have a special time set aside to honor all the children through 12th grade and college students for their achievements. Also consider giving special recognition to the seniors 65 and older. If your family does not have family reunions, perhaps you and another family member can begin one, or start planning events where everyone meets for dinner or attends a play once a year, or organize birthday celebrations four times year.

Make a commitment to do something that will bring your family together and also include someone who does not have a family.

_____

_____

_____

FAITH "AT CENTER" VS. FAITH "OFF-CENTER"

1 Samuel 1:1-28

"Therefore confess your sins to each other and pray for each other so that you may be healed. The prayer of a righteous man is powerful and effective" (James 5:16, NIV).

Lesson Focus: God's Family Prays—Hannah desperately needed something from God. She understood the power of prayer and went about seeking God in a way that she knew would gain God's attention. Hannah demonstrated her faith as she set her focus on communicating with God. Not only did she pray with intensity, Hannah also made a vow to God that she indeed kept. It would serve us well to follow Hannah's example and to go before the Lord in this most powerful way; for it is through our earnest prayers that God will hear our hearts and respond accordingly.

Words and Phrases You Should Know

In preparation for the lesson, familiarize yourself with the following definitions:
- **Faith**—Trust in God to provide for us (without seeing or knowing how God will resolve the matter)
- **Prayer**—Communication with God
- **Efficacy**—Capacity for producing a desired result or effect

LIFE APPLICATION DISCUSSION QUESTIONS

State your own personal views in answering the following questions.

Take a moment to pray for strength to keep the faith and trust God at all times.

1. Are there ministries or programs in the church and your community that will help to foster relationships between mother and son/daughter and father and son/daughter? List the programs and any other additional contact information. Write a sentence to describe the program as well. Have someone compile the information and give to the church office as a resource guide for church members and the community.

_____

_____

_____

2. When was the last time you doubted God and did not do what the Lord asked you to do? Describe the circumstances and the consequences that occurred after your decision to do it **your** way.

_____

_____

_____

3. Write out your definition for the words "faith" and "trust." What are the similarities or differences?

_____

_____

_____

BIBLE APPLICATION EXERCISES

1. A Closer Look at Prayer

Learning to trust God's Word and to have faith in God takes time and can be very challenging for us. Hannah's burden of not having a son was greater than the knowledge that her husband, Elkanah, loved her more than he loved Peninnah. Her frustration, anger, and feelings of abandonment had reached a boiling point. Hannah cried out in prayer with the anguish of someone who needs God to respond *right now*. Waiting on the Lord had been extremely painful for Hannah. But Hannah's cry for a son was heard and answered by the Lord. God honored her desire to have a child and faithfully give him back to the Lord for service.

Read the following Scriptures to determine if they have provided guidance for you when you were waiting for the Lord in faith, but were also frustrated. Record your thoughts.

a. God gives strength to the weary (Isaiah 40:29-31)

_____

_____

b. Do not worry about your life (Matthew 6:25-34)

_____

_____

c. Daniel in the lion's den (Daniel 6)

_____

_____

d. The woman with the blood disease (Matthew 9:18-26)

_____

_____

e. Lost younger son/disgruntled elder son (Luke 15:28-31)

_____

_____

Personal Application

1. Think of the family that was presented in the introductory story of chapter 4 and your own family. Reflect on any similar situations in your family. Pray and ask God to heal those who have been wounded by life and find it difficult to overcome their struggles. Also thank God for those who are experiencing God's victory in their lives.

_____

_____

_____

2. Did a family situation of which you are aware have a happy ending as the one presented in the introductory story? Write out your response to the ending of the story. Do you think circumstances work out so nicely in real life? Explain your answer during class discussion and in writing out your response.

_____

_____

_____

3. Share how other believers in Christ provided encouragement or support for the family's situation as it was being worked out.

_____

_____

_____

2. Why Pray?
Communicating with God through prayer brings results. It is the way that the Spirit of God directs our comings and goings. In times of dilemma, we can receive the answers we need from God through prayer. After reading the following Scripture passages, tell whether these biblical characters used wisdom through prayer in their situations. If not, what advice would you have given them? Answers will vary, but some possible answers are:

    a. Peter at Jesus' Arrest (Luke 22:48-51)

_____

_____

    b. The Rich Young Man (Luke 18:18-25)

_____

_____

    c. Hannah's Prayer (1 Samuel 2:1-11)

_____

_____

Personal Application
Read the following statements and write your thoughts in the space provided. Include some Scriptures in support of how you respond.

Relationships can become very strained on many different levels when one person feels less important than another, or knows that someone else receives more favor. Hannah and Peninnah both had such issues. Their husband Elkanah showed that he loved Hannah more than Peninnah, but Peninnah had his children. Peninnah knew that she was not loved by Elkanah as Hannah was, so she made Hannah's life miserable whenever she had the chance. Hannah allowed herself to feel tortured and inferior because she felt that God was not blessing her with a child.

_____

_____

_____

3. Being a Part of the Solution

The Peninnah, Hannah, Elkanah moments in your life can be from childhood events until the present moment. To share with the group, write out your testimonies for times when you have personally experienced the following:

- a Peninnah moment: the bully or perpetrator of mean ideas or words directed toward someone else
- a Hannah moment: first a victim, then a victor
- an Elkanah moment: a caring person, but feeling helpless and caught in the middle

_____

_____

_____

Read the following Scriptures and include them as you write your testimonies of how prayer and trusting God's Word changed a situation for the better.

a. "Though he slay me, yet will I trust in him" (Job 13:15).

_____

_____

b. "The Lord is my light and my salvation" (Psalm 27:1)

_____

_____

c. "Whatsoever things are of good report. . ." (Philippians 4:8)

_____

_____

d. "I can do all things through Christ who strengthens me" (Philippians 4:13)

_____

_____

Personal Application
Reread the story of Hannah in 1 Samuel chapter 1, and imagine yourself in her place. Write your own scenario. You may want to change the need for a child to whatever need you may have in your life. Now pray and have the faith and patience to wait on the Lord for an answer to your prayer. Remember, the Lord does not always answer us when and how we want, but be prepared to wait for and accept God's answer.

_____

_____

_____

The Family Ties Commitment Activity
Make a list of four to five parents that you know in your extended family, friends, or community; include grandparents, aunts, and others who have stepped in to serve as parents. List each name separately on your sheet. Beside each name, write a word that represents what you know they may need through prayer. Pray for peace, love, or other blessings that will help the individual and their families. Write this list twice a week for a month, and include the children of the parents at this time, or in the following month.

PARENTS:

_____

_____

_____

_____

_____

CHILDREN OF THE PARENTS:

_____

_____

_____

_____

_____

UNITING VS. FRAGMENTING

Daniel 3:1, 4-6, 16-23, 26-28

Jesus answered, "It is written: 'Worship the Lord your God and serve him only'" (Luke 4:8, NIV).

Lesson Focus: God's Family Worships—Standing together for a belief or a cause that is built upon the foundation of the Lord can open the door for persecution and for suffering. But, as Christians, we are to stand as the three young Hebrew men did. It may cost us our lives, but we are to stand for God. In the tradition of these young men, we have learned invaluable lessons from our foreparents and leaders such as Rosa Parks and Thurgood Marshall. In their honor, we must stand on the honesty and truth that the Lord has given us. Worshiping other gods and allowing them to take precedence over Christ as the head of our lives, sets us up for trouble and confusion, and prevents us from fully living out what the Lord would have us to do. Although the Hebrew men were enslaved by King Nebuchadnezzar, they held on to their pride, dignity, and belief in God.

Words and Phrases You Should Know
In preparation for the lesson, familiarize yourself with the following definitions:
- **Daniel**—Means "God is my judge" in Hebrew
- **Belteshazzar**—Means "lord of the straightened's treasure" in Hebrew
- **Hananiah**—Means "God has favored" in Hebrew
- **Shadrach**—Means "royal" or "the great scribe" in Hebrew
- **Mishael**—Means "who is like God" in Hebrew
- **Meshach**—Means "guest of a king" in Hebrew
- **Azariah**—Means "Jehovah has helped" in Hebrew
- **Abednego**—Means "servant of Nebo" in Hebrew
- **Nebuchadnezzar**—Means "may Nebo protect the crown" in Hebrew
- **Refugee**—"one that flees for refuge or safety, especially to a foreign country as in times of political upheaval, war, etc."

LIFE APPLICATION DISCUSSION QUESTIONS
State your own personal views in answering the following questions.

1. Examine your understanding of what it means to worship God. What are the ways in which we offer true worship to God? Are you fulfilling God's purpose for creating you by offering God your genuine worship?

_____

_____

_____

2. Are there any similarities between the three young Hebrew men standing up for what they believed in and the bombing of the church in Birmingham, Alabama, where four young girls died?

_____

_____

_____

3. What are some of the ways that your church and your family welcome new persons and interact with those who may have different opinions or ways of doing things?

_____

_____

_____

4. Are there any messages or lessons that we can learn from the young men in this story that apply to the young men in our church, families, and in the community?

_____

_____

_____

5. Are there any messages or lessons that our young ladies can learn from the young men in this story?

_____

_____

_____

6. Are there any messages or lessons that our pastors and other church leaders can learn from the young men in this story?

_____

_____

_____

BIBLE APPLICATION EXERCISES

1. A Closer Look

In this story, anger, courage, death, violence, multiple egos, and God's divine intervention are very real and alive. Their willingness to totally trust the Lord for deliverance or not, echoes a hard reality that many of us are not willing to face today. Their stand speaks clearly to the fact that they worshiped God above all else—even above their very lives.

a. Review the following verses. In your own words, express how you feel Jesus would address the issues in the Scriptures.
1) Acts 5:1-5

_____

_____

2) Acts 5:10

_____

_____

3) Acts 5:25-28

_____

_____

b. Why do you think God spared the lives of the Hebrew young men?

_____

_____

c. When you reread Daniel chapter 3, note that you do not see Jesus mentioned by name as one of those in the fiery furnace. Do you believe that it was Jesus, or maybe a figment of their imagination? Why or why not? Support your answer with the Scriptures and not your opinion.

_____

_____

d. As you review Daniel chapter 3, identify the reason(s) why the Hebrew boys were willing to sacrifice their lives for God.

_____

_____

Personal Application

1. Read the chapter 5 introductory story and Scripture passage again and describe the various characters and their egos. How do you see God working within these characters?

_____

_____

_____

2. A wonderful poet named, Nikki Giovanni, wrote a poem called "Ego Tripping." She expresses in this poem the grandeur and significance of one woman's ego. We discover that "ego tripping" has been a part of humanity since the beginning of time. Sometimes God has to bring our egos into submission and remind us that we can do nothing without Him. We are called to worship and serve God alone. In your family, are there those whose egos need checking? What Scriptures will help to keep us focused on God and not allow our egos (Edging God Out) to keep us from serving the Lord in an excellent way?

_____

2. The Hebrew Boys Worshiped Only the One True God

If the young men did not worship the other gods, they would surely face death. Yet, they were not moved by the threat of death. What a strong testimony to their faith as they declared loyalty to God and would not submit before the king. Some people are able to stand up for what they believe in and do not fear death. Read the following Scriptures and write how a strong faith is expressed or exercised. Answers will vary.

a. Daniel 6:19-22

_____

_____

b. Genesis 6:14-22

_____

_____

c. Mark 14:32-36

_____

_____

d. Luke 13:10-14

_____

_____

Personal Application

1. "You shall have no other gods before me," (Exodus 20:3, KJV). What are the gods that you see in the community that have affected your personal relationship with Christ and how you serve as a disciple?

_____

_____

_____

2. When was the last time your immediate and extended families attended church together and rededicated their lives to Christ? If this is the first time, make this a special event with pictures, videos, and other special moments that will preserve this memory. Discuss the event or the possibility.

_____

_____

_____

3. Being a Part of the Solution

As a family, decide if there are things that are often placed before attending church or doing what you know is right before the Lord. Make a list of those things that have taken first place before serving God. Then make a commitment for one month to not allow these things to take precedence over attending a worship service or any other church activity where you can serve the Lord.

_____

_____

_____

Personal Application

"You shall not make for yourself an idol in the form of anything in heaven above or on the earth beneath or in the waters below," (Exodus 20:4).

1. Write about what this Scripture means to you personally.

_____

_____

_____

2. Is there anything preventing you from worshiping God with your entire being? Make a list and pray about it in your daily devotion time with the Lord.

_____

_____

_____

The Family Ties Commitment Activity

Plan a barbeque or other family outing and invite seniors and others in the church who either have no family or limited access to their families. Allow the children to plan a program and offer a prayer of care and commitment to serve the Lord first. Make a list of whom to invite and brainstorm ideas for something special that you would like to give to them.

_____

_____

_____

_____

_____

INVESTING VS. WASTING

Mark 12:38-44

"Give, and it will be given to you. A good measure, pressed down, shaken together and running over, will be poured into your lap. For with the measure you use, it will be measured to you" (Luke 6:38, NIV).

Lesson Focus: God's Family Gives—Why is it that poor people often have a better spirit of giving than rich people? It is important that we all practice and have within us the spirit of giving out of the abundance of our hearts. Holding on to what we have or only doing things in church for show are not acceptable behaviors before Jesus. Teaching and setting examples of how to save and how to give are important lessons for us all. The widow was not afraid to give and to have nothing left over. We may sing that we "would rather have Jesus than silver and gold," but our actions do not always reflect this. A giving heart and spirit reflect God's giving and caring spirit toward us. As we are willing to give out of love and obedience to God, giving is an outward expression of where we are inwardly in our faith walk.

Words and Phrases You Should Know
In preparation for the lesson, familiarize yourself with the following definitions. (All definitions are from *Random House Webster's Unabridged Dictionary*. New York: Random House, 1998.)
- **Racism**—A belief that inherent differences among the various members of the human race determine cultural or individual achievement, usually involving the idea that one's own race is superior and has the right to rule over another.
- **Class-ism**—A biased or discriminatory attitude based on distinctions made between social or economic classes.
- **Justice**—The quality of being just; righteousness, equitableness, or moral rightness.

LIFE APPLICATION DISCUSSION QUESTIONS
State your own personal views in answering the following questions.

1. Do you think Jesus is against persons being rich? Why? Why not?

   _____

   _____

   _____

2. In your present financial state, if you had more money, how would your life change personally and for your family?

   _____

   _____

   _____

3. Do you think persons should include their respective church in their will?

   _____

_____

_____

4. Why do you think there are so many poor people in the world?

_____

_____

_____

5. How is your church and your family addressing the issues associated with poverty?

_____

_____

_____

BIBLE APPLICATION EXERCISES

1. Giving from a Willing Heart

Read and write how you understand the attitude and actions in the Scriptures below.

　　a. Luke 16:13-15 (keeping good public appearances)

_____

_____

　　b. John 11:21-22, 32-35 (Mary and Martha)

_____

_____

　　c. John 13:2-5 (foot washing)

_____

_____

　　d. Acts 16:25-28 (Paul and Silas)

_____

_____

Personal Application

1. If Jesus joined your family for dinner today, what would you do differently, and how much money and time would you spend to impress Him?

_____

_____

2. If the pastor or church leader joined your family for dinner today, how much time and money would you spend in preparing for your guests? Why?

_____

_____

_____

3. Do you give to other organizations or persons who are in need? If yes, how often, and what do you donate? On what Scriptures do you base your reasons for giving and what is your attitude when you are giving?

_____

_____

_____

2. The Widow's Mite
Through various Scripture references, we see that Jesus wanted [or warned] the rich to not flaunt their wealth by making a display of their financial blessings. He also challenged how the rich made their money and shared their wealth. Read the following verses and share how you understand God's view of the poor.

a. Luke 4:18

_____

_____

b. Luke 18:22-25

_____

_____

c. Mark 14:6-9

_____

_____

d. Mark 12:41-44

_____

_____

e. Matthew 5:3

_____

_____

f. Ecclesiastes 5:8-9

_____

_____

g. Ecclesiastes 5:10

_____

_____

_____

Personal Application

1. Why is "poverty" a global reality?

_____

_____

2. How do you address the issues of poverty within your community, city, or in the world?

_____

_____

3. What is the church's responsibility to address issues of poverty and greed?

_____

_____

4. How does your family cope with or address matters of poverty? Are there family members that work together to help those who are financially in need?

_____

_____

3. Being a Part of the Solution

Many young minds are going to waste because there are not enough mentors and others who are willing to invest their time and money into helping these youths to overcome poverty: poverty of body, mind, and spirit. Many of these youths do not want to work manual labor. Why do you think manual labor is not valued as a high-paying job? Why should mentors encourage young people to perform manual labor as a means of advancement?

_____

_____

_____

Personal Application

1. List three reasons why you believe owners of sports teams and various movie stars are paid more than teachers, secretaries, and nurses?

_____

_____

_____

2. Now ask family members to go on a fast from a material item that they desire (this may include food items), but do not need for four days. Each person may keep a journal or create something that expresses their thoughts and feelings during their fast. The fast may also involve doing something for the greater good of others or self, (e.g., exercising, not smoking).

Family Ties Commitment Activity

As a family, have conversations on how to advocate laws that will help those with healthcare needs or housing. Offer your support by working with a local organization to protest against inadequate healthcare and housing for poor and low-income residents. If there are many poor persons either in your community or one nearby, work with the local shelters and schools to start a clothing or school supplies drive. Within your church and your family, dedicate a special time to lift up the needs and the hearts of the poor around the world, and write a prayer asking the Lord for insight as to what you should do and how you can make a difference in helping the poor.

_____

_____

_____

_____

_____

_____

Amen.

RITES OF PASSAGE
(RESPECTING VS. DISRESPECTING)

Luke 2:41-52

"Children, obey your parents in the Lord, for this is right" (Ephesians 6:1, NIV).

Lesson Focus: God's Family Obeys—God places a very high value on the family unit and parents teaching His commands or statutes to generations to come. He expects each generation to establish a personal relationship with Him and in order to do so, the generation before has to do its part to share their wisdom and experience, and transmit the laws, customs, and traditions to their offspring. Rites of Passage are about respecting the next generation. It is about preparing them to successfully assume their leadership roles in living for and worshiping a God who loved them so much, that He was willing to send His only Son to pay their sin-penalty so that they could live with Him eternally.

Words and Phrases You Should Know
In preparation for the lesson, familiarize yourself with the following definitions:

- **Respecting**—Esteeming or valuing one's personhood—who he or she is and what he or she has accomplished in life; to hold in high regard
- **Disrespecting**—Devaluing one's personhood—who he/she is and what he/she has accomplished in life; to hold in low regard
- **Rites of Passage Programs**—Activities designed to teach a certain age group of boys or girls the norms and value of the society, God, and the Bible, and what it means to live and walk as men and women of God
- **Feelings of abandonment**—A mind-set of being left alone, forsaken, deserted
- **Feelings of alienation**—A mind-set of being excluded or of not being a part of a group; estranged; detached
- **Healthy self-esteem**—Valuing oneself as a person and as a child of God; having regard or respect for oneself
- **Low self-esteem**—Having a low self-worth as a person and as a child of God; low self-respect

LIFE APPLICATION DISCUSSION QUESTIONS
State your own personal views in answering the following questions.

1. How can the church, through "Rites of Passage" programs, help the Black community to build stronger family ties?

_____

_____

_____

2. List some social agencies that might come alongside to help in developing a "Rite of Passage" program at your church, and how might the listed agencies help you?

_____

_____

_____

3. Why is it paramount that young boys or men have other men as positive role models?

_____

_____

_____

4. Why is it paramount that young girls or women have other women as positive role models?

_____

_____

_____

BIBLE APPLICATION EXERCISES

1. A Closer Look

Feelings of abandonment, alienation, being lost, and being found were some of the themes that ran through many of the testimonies of the boys and men in the chapter 7 introductory story. However, Jesus had a very positive attitude toward children. In fact, He says that one must become like a little child in order to enter His kingdom. Review the following verses and in your own words, express what Jesus is saying about the respect we should have for children or the warnings against disrespecting them.

a. Matthew 18:10

_____

_____

b. Mark 10:14-16

_____

_____

c. Luke 1:66

_____

_____

d. Ephesians 6:1-3

_____

_____

e. Ephesians 6:4

_____

Personal Application

1. How can knowing about Jesus' positive attitude toward children help you enhance your own family ties, or let go of some childhood hurts that may have impacted your life?

_____

_____

_____

2. How can knowing about Jesus' positive attitude toward children help you reach out to someone else (perhaps a child in your own family) who has a poor self-image?

_____

_____

_____

2. The Boy Jesus in the Temple (Jesus and His Earthly Parents)

It was customary in the Jewish society for children to be taught both at home and at the temple or synagogue. At age 12, Jesus would have already been receiving instruction in the Law of Moses, perhaps in a local synagogue. Read the following verses and record how studying and applying these statutes to your life can help enhance your own family ties.

    a. Deuteronomy 4:1

_____

_____

    b. Deuteronomy 4:9

_____

_____

    c. Deuteronomy 6:1-2

_____

_____

    d. Deuteronomy 6:5-6

_____

_____

    e. Romans 6:1-2

_____

_____

f. Romans 8:6

_____

_____

Personal Application

1. "Do not follow other gods, the gods of the peoples around you" (Deuteronomy 6:14). List some of the "other" gods that have weakened family ties in your own biological or church family.

_____

_____

_____

2. "In the future, when your son asks you, 'What is the meaning of the stipulations, decrees and laws the LORD our God has commanded you?' tell him: "We were slaves of Pharaoh in Egypt, but the LORD brought us out of Egypt with a mighty hand'" (Deuteronomy 6:20-21). Write a brief synopsis that could be used to share with a young person of how God brought African Americans out of slavery with a mighty hand.

_____

_____

_____

_____

3. Being a Part of the Solution

As children of Almighty God, we should be a part of the solution rather than part of the problems we experience in both our biological and church families. To facilitate unity in both, we must find practical answers to the problems. The poem on page 37 offers some suggestions of how we can enhance family unity. Using some of the solutions offered in the poem below, take any one of the characters in the introductory story and tell what you might do to bless, encourage, lighten a heavy load, or help heal a heart. Answers will vary.

THE FAMILY OF GOD
We are the family of God
Striving to see His face by and by,
Yes, hoping to meet our Heavenly Father
One glorious day in the sky.

May I encourage you
As we travel on our way,
Or lighten the load you carry
On a very trying day.

And when I have a day of spiritual anguish,
Will you take me before our God,
And pray for all I need,
To bless and heal my heart?
—Evangeline Carey

_____
_____
_____

Personal Application
It is so easy to point out what others can do to alleviate some of the problems plaguing many Black families. However, what can you personally do to heal any rifts in your own family or church?

_____
_____
_____
_____

The Family Ties Commitment Activity
Make a commitment to pray for families (saved and unsaved) across this country and the world. Include in your prayer the salvation of unsaved coworkers, friends, and loved ones. Write your prayer.

_____
_____
_____
_____
_____

Amen.

BEING RESPONSIBLE VS. BEING IRRESPONSIBLE

Luke 10:30-37

"For we are God's workmanship, created in Christ Jesus to do good works, which God prepared in advance for us to do" (Ephesians 2:10, NIV).

Lesson Focus: God's Family Does Good Works—Family should be about bonding and loving unconditionally, in spite of who does not measure up to the standards set by the family, who cannot pull themselves up "by their own bootstraps," or who does not even have "bootstraps" to pull themselves up. Family is about inclusiveness; that is, including even those who have been or are being irresponsible with their own lives. In fact, these may be the very ones who need our loving attention the most. This requires doing good works within the family as God has designed His people to do.

Words and Phrases You Should Know

In preparation for the lesson, familiarize yourself with the following definitions:

- **Family unity**—Family members helping and loving each other unconditionally, regardless of which members are deemed by the unit as responsible or irresponsible
- **Being our brother's keeper**—Tangibly looking out for and unconditionally loving members of our family and beyond, even when they cannot give us back anything in return
- **A holy reunion**—Inviting all members of the family to the reunion table by having those who are affluent help those who need our support to attend
- **Nuclear family**—Usually consists of father, mother, brothers, and sisters or some derivation thereof
- **Extended family**—The family extends outwardly to include aunts, uncles, cousins, and other relatives
- **Accumulated wealth**—Assets including money, stocks and bonds, property, etc., over and above what is needed for everyday living
- **Family affirmation**—Validating, applauding, accepting family members who by society's definition are considered failures, loving them in spite of, and caring for them even though they find it difficult to care for themselves

LIFE APPLICATION DISCUSSION QUESTIONS

State your own personal views in answering the following questions:

1. What are some ways that families distinguish between the "haves" and the "have not(s)" within the family?

_____

_____

_____

2. What practical ways can family members help other members who are irresponsible with their own personal lives?

_____

_____

_____

3. What can churches do to encourage irresponsible members of the body to be more responsible in their own lives?

_____

_____

_____

4. Are there times when a responsible family member should refuse to help an irresponsible member? Why? Why not?

_____

_____

_____

BIBLE APPLICATION EXERCISES

1. How God Feels about the Poor

When there are members of the nuclear or extended family that are left behind as others climb the proverbial middle-class ladder, there can be mega-strain in family relationships. This can also be true in the body of Christ, especially when members equate being poor or financially challenged with the degree of one's faith. Unfortunately, some members of the body of Christ do label other members and treat them accordingly. Review the following verses and in your own words express how God feels about the poor.

   a. Psalm 41:1

_____

_____

   b. Psalm 72:4

_____

_____

   c. Proverbs 14:21

_____

_____

   d. Proverbs 14:31

_____

_____

e. Proverbs 22:2

_____

_____

f. Isaiah 11:1-4

_____

_____

Personal Application
1. Have you ever been poor and needy? Relate your personal experience and write out your testimony.

_____

_____

_____

2. Have you ever reached out to someone else who was poor and needy? How did you help?

_____

_____

_____

2. The Good Samaritan
The Good Samaritan was "good" because he reached down to help his fallen brother, even though that brother was of a race that considered themselves superior to his. (The Jews did not have any dealings with the Samaritans, who had intermarried with their Jewish captors or enemies). Take the priest and the Levite from the Bible story, and in your own words, tell what their real issues were—what prevented them from helping their needy brother?

    a. The priest:

_____

_____

    b. The Levite:

_____

_____

Personal Application
1. In your own words, how did the "Good Samaritan" represent Jesus Christ?

_____

_____

2. How is it possible that the two religious leaders failed to help their brother when their roles were to represent Christ in their religious order?

_____

_____

_____

3. Bridging the Economic Divide in Families

There is often an economic divide in both biological and church families. In fact, the economic scale can range from "poor and always needy" all the way to "rich." The disparities can cause a split within the family, if family members allow it.

What can the church do to pull down the walls of division (which is a way of performing good works) along socio-economic lines in the body of Christ?

_____

_____

_____

Personal Application

List the first name of a needy member of your biological or church family. Then make a list of ways or things you personally could do to meet some of his or her needs. Finally, take action by showing that you are willing to do the good works that God has placed before you.

_____

_____

_____

The Family Ties Commitment Activity

Note some of the important things that you have learned from this lesson on doing good works, which can be summed up as "Being Responsible vs. Being Irresponsible." Pray for guidance about choosing to do some good works that will help your personal and church family members.

_____

_____

_____

CREATING FAMILY VS. EXISTING IN A VACUUM

John 1:45-51

"I pray that you may be active in sharing your faith, so that you will have a full understanding of every good thing we have in Christ" (Philemon 1:6, NIV).

Lesson Focus: God's Family Witnesses—What is the business of the church? In His mandate—"The Great Commission," Jesus tells believers to "Go and make disciples of all nations, baptizing them in the name of the Father and of the Son and of the Holy Spirit, and teaching them to obey everything I have commanded you" (Matthew 28:19-20). Even though the church is often busy planning anniversaries, musicals, dinners, etc., the real calling of the church is to carry out God's kingdom building initiative. We are to take Jesus' message everywhere, even to the ghettoes of America.

Words and Phrases You Should Know
In preparation for the lesson, familiarize yourself with the following definitions:
- **Commuter members of the church**—Members living outside of the church's immediate neighborhood
- **Support the church**—Giving time, tithes, offerings, and talents to the church
- **Youth programs**—Programs instituted by the church to minister to the physical and spiritual needs of young people
- **Vacation Bible School (VBS)**—A church-sponsored Bible school program, usually held one to two weeks during the summer months, with an outreach program to the surrounding neighborhoods. The objective is to teach God's Word
- **Faithful members**—Members who attend and support the church through attendance, finances, and service
- **Black flight**—Blacks fleeing the inner-city to take up residence in the surrounding suburbs

LIFE APPLICATION DISCUSSION QUESTIONS
State your own personal views in answering the following questions:

1. Who is God concerned about outside of the body of Christ?

_____

_____

_____

2. Can "good" youth leaders be found in "bad" neighborhoods? Why? Why not?

_____

_____

_____

3. Should the church pursue and witness to gangsters and junkies? Why? Why not?

_____

_____

_____

4. Should churches strive to be only in "good" neighborhoods? Why? Why not?

_____

_____

_____

5. What is the real purpose of the church?

_____

_____

_____

BIBLE APPLICATION EXERCISES

1. In Which Neighborhood Should God's Church Be Found? Why?

Some churches feel that once their members move on to better, upper-class neighborhoods, that the church also needs to relocate. They cannot see that they can have a viable ministry in the crime-ridden, lower-class neighborhood where they are located. However, God is looking for ministers to transcend socio-economic lines and share His Good News wherever people have spiritual and material needs, and as a result, experience much hurt and pain.

    a. In John 1:46, what did Nathanael really mean by "Can anything good come from there [Nazareth]?"

_____

_____

_____

    b. List the names of a few "successful" people that you know, who have come out of "Nazareth-like" backgrounds (ghettoes or economically-deprived areas) and include their areas of success.

        1) _____

        2) _____

        3) _____

        4) _____

        5) _____

c. Fill in the missing words in Matthew 28:19-20 (NIV), or write out these verses in the Bible version that you have and highlight the words that indicate an "action" must be taken.

"Therefore _____ and _____ disciples of _____ nations, _____ them in the name of the _____ and of the _____ and of the _____ _____, and _____ them to _____ everything I have _____ you."

Personal Application

1. Study Matthew 28:19-20 and write an explanation of what it means to you personally.

_____

_____

_____

2. At the end of the introductory story of chapter 9, Brother Watkins said that "Jesus was not called to save people who are well. He came to take care of those who were sick." Is this your understanding of why Jesus came? Why? Why not?

_____

_____

_____

3. Are the approximately 300 Black mega churches and thousands of smaller ones located across the U.S. really impacting the Black inner-city pain and suffering that is shown in rising crime and drug infested areas, insufficient health care, high underemployment and unemployment, and antiquated educational infrastructures that produce underperforming schools? Explain.

_____

_____

_____

2. A Closer Look at the Church's Calling

There is no doubt that the lower-class, crime-ridden neighborhoods surrounding our churches pose numerous challenges that God wants to meet through the work of faithful believers in the local church. Therefore, God expects the members of His church to be the "salt of the earth and the light of the world" and lift Him up so that we can do our part in building God's kingdom.

a. What are some of the challenges posed by the neighborhoods surrounding your church?

_____

_____

_____

b. What seems to be the reason for the existence of your church? Is your church meeting the description Jesus gave of His followers in Matthew 5:13-14?

_____

_____

_____

Personal Application

1. In what outreach programs is your church involved?

_____

_____

_____

2. How can you help your church in its outreach programs?

_____

_____

3. Being a Part of the Solution

Some churches are getting involved in politics (through lobbying and giving support to Christian candidates to run for office, etc.), so that they can really impact the surrounding lower-class, crime-ridden communities. These churches appreciate and know that without a power base, change will be slow or nonexistent.

To help solve many of the problems plaguing lower-class Black communities, should the church be involved in politics? Why? Why not?

_____

_____

_____

_____

_____

Personal Application

Would you be willing to run for a political office? Why? Why not?

_____

_____

_____

_____

_____

The Family Ties Commitment Activity

God has called all believers to help Him build His kingdom that will consist of every blood-washed one; that is, everyone who has believed on the Lord Jesus Christ as their personal Savior. God does not want His church to exist in a vacuum, but rather to increase by the witness and testimonies of those who belong to the family of God.

Note some of the important things that you have learned from this lesson about "Creating Family vs. Existing in a Vacuum." Pray for guidance on how to apply what you've learned to your personal situation.

_____

_____

_____

_____

_____

THE FAMILY REUNION: WITH GOD VS. WITHOUT GOD

Revelation 21:1-7

"But in keeping with his promise we are looking forward to a new heaven and a new earth, the home of righteousness" (2 Peter 3:13, NIV).

Lesson Focus: God's Family Celebrates—The kingdom of God will replace the evil world system of greed and selfishness, and God will make all things new, including a new and eternal heaven and Earth (Revelation 21:1). In his vision while exiled on the island of Patmos in the Aegean Sea, the apostle John saw a new Jerusalem (the new city of God) where God lives among His people. This new Jerusalem is a picture of God's future home for believers (God's people). Because God reigns in the holy city, there is love, peace, and security. The evil, pain, and suffering that we now know will come to an end. God will remove all sorrow and the redeemed (every blood-washed believer) will be invited to dwell with Him there forever and ever. Jesus, the humble, suffering servant, is also the conquering, powerful King of kings and Lord of lords who brings comfort, hope, and salvation to His people.

Words and Phrases You Should Know
In preparation for the lesson, familiarize yourself with the following definitions:
- **Looking for love in all the wrong places**—Usually denotes searching for someone to love you by having intimate relationships with numerous partners, only to be disappointed
- **A family unity that is empowered by the Holy Spirit of God**—Relying on God through His Holy Spirit to repair the breaches or disunity within the family unit
- **Spiritual warfare**—Daily standing against the vicious attacks and schemes of Satan by putting on the whole armor of God, which includes: "truth, righteousness, the gospel of peace, faith, the helmet of salvation, and the word of God (see Ephesians 6:14-17). In battling Satan, "we wrestle not against flesh and blood, but against principalities, against powers, against the rulers of the darkness of this world, against spiritual wickedness in high places" (vv. 11-12, KJV).

LIFE APPLICATION DISCUSSION QUESTIONS
State your own personal views in answering the following questions:

1. Do you agree with those who view the world system as impersonal, and within this system, for the most part, people are mere commodities? Why or why not?

_____

_____

_____

2. Summarize how African Americans, both as individuals and as families, have been impacted by the world's system?

_____

_____

_____

3. Discuss what it means to you that in God's family/kingdom, one person is not valued over another, but all are valued equally.

_____

_____

_____

4. Name some careers that you feel build up families and strengthen the Black community.

_____

_____

5. How can churches help to teach God's view of the value of each human being?

_____

_____

_____

BIBLE APPLICATION EXERCISES
1. "The Great Family Reunion"
Family reunions can be very happy occasions. They provide an opportunity for family members to renew relationships and forge ahead to brighter tomorrows through showing love and helping each other. God made every human being to be a part of a family: His spiritual family, which is called, "the body of Christ." Within His holy Word are guidelines for family membership and how we are to treat one another.

Look at 1 Corinthians 13:1-8 and state, in your own words, God's principles for loving one another.

1 Corinthians 13:1

_____

_____

_____

verse 2

_____

_____

_____

verse 3

_____

_____

_____

verses 4–7

_____

_____

_____

verse 8

_____

_____

_____

Personal Application

1. Have you ever looked for love in all the wrong places as Ann did in the chapter 10 introductory story? If so, share how God delivered you. If not, share how God delivered a friend or loved one who has been through a similar experience.

_____

_____

_____

_____

_____

2. How can you personally come alongside and help someone who is looking for love in all the wrong places?

_____

_____

_____

_____

_____

2. The New Heaven and the New Earth

Evil, injustice, pain, suffering, tears, and violence are very much a part of the way in which the world operates. These negative elements have been fuelled by greed and selfishness. However, the victorious, conquering King of kings and Lord of lords is going to put an end to the evil practices of the world. At Jesus' Second Coming, God is prepared to usher in His own personal system and defeat evil and Satan.

Read and explain what Revelation 21:4 will mean for many believers who have suffered inequality, injustice, and violence in this world's system.

_____

_____

_____

_____

_____

_____

Personal Application

Read and explain what Revelation 21:6 means to you personally.

_____

_____

_____

3. Being a Part of the Solution

The world's system is based on selfishness and greed. In fact, many people have lost their self-respect and Christian values as they compromised with the wicked ways of the world.

a. What are some of the challenges posed by the neighborhoods surrounding your church because of the world's system?

_____

_____

_____

b. How is your church helping those who have been marginalized by the world's system?

_____

_____

_____

Personal Application

1. In what outreach programs are you involved that serve to help those who have been disenfranchised and marginalized by the world's system?

_____

_____

_____

2. How can you help family members who have been disenfranchised by the world's system and bring them spiritual enlightenment about God's system that is based on love, forgiveness, and obedience?

_____

_____

_____

The Family Ties Commitment Activity

A family reunion with God is very different from one without Him. In fact, it has some very distinct characteristics.

Note some of the important things that you have learned from this lesson on "The Family Reunion: With God vs. Without God." Pray for guidance on how to apply them to your personal family situation.

_____

_____

_____

_____

_____

_____

MAKING PEACE VS. MAKING WAR

2 Samuel 3:7-8; 21:1-14

"David asked the Gibeonites, 'What shall I do for you? How shall I make amends so that you will bless the LORD's inheritance?'" (2 Samuel 21:3, NIV).

Lesson Focus: God's Family Lives Peacefully—Often years of hurt and nurturing grudges can take a negative toll on families. Many have found the chasm left by these grudges to be so wide that the family becomes dysfunctional. In the key verse, David wanted to tear down the walls that hindered his people's blessings from God. He wanted to make amends to the Gibeonites—a remnant of Amorites that Israel had sworn not to destroy (Joshua 9:16-20). However, King Saul tried to wipe them out years before. Now, in order to rid the family of the consequences of Saul's broken vow to the Gibeonites, Saul's sons had to make amends for the murders that their father had committed.

Words and Phrases You Should Know
To better understand the lesson, there are certain phrases that you should know. Read or display the following definitions and allow time for discussion.
- **Defending the neighborhood**—Looking out for and enhancing the good of the neighborhood; looking after the neighborhood's well being
- **Exacerbating negative situations**—Using political power and economic resources or a lack thereof to destroy the fabric of the neighborhood
- **Scarce resources**—Necessities needed for the members of a neighborhood or society to thrive and survive are limited or non-existent, (i.e., affordable housing, jobs, accessible health care, etc.)
- **Celebrate life**—Placing a high value on God-given life itself, including all resources: people, nature, property, which all belong to God
- **Spiritual values**—Biblical standards, morals, principles governing daily behavior and living; loving and obeying God, loving our fellowman, being our brother's keeper

LIFE APPLICATION DISCUSSION QUESTIONS
State your own personal views in answering the following questions:

1. List some of the deep-festering hurts that plague many African American families.

_____

_____

2. What can the church do to promote peace and reconciliation in African American families and to help alleviate the devastation that economic and political factors have had on them?

_____

_____

3. What can the church do to enhance peace and reconciliation within the church family?

_____

_____

4. How can churches help to bring much needed jobs to African American communities?

_____

_____

5. What are some specific things we can pray that God will do to heal deep-seated family hurts both inside and outside of the church?

_____

_____

BIBLE APPLICATION EXERCISES
1. No Division in God's Family
Division in the family of God sends a dubious or hypocritical message to a lost and dying world. For the church to be an effective witness for Jesus Christ, unbelievers need to recognize the church by her unconditional love for individuals and families alike. Review the following verses and restate their truths in your own words.

a. 1 Corinthians 1:10

_____

_____

b. 2 Corinthians 1:3-4

_____

_____

c. Romans 15:5-6

_____

_____

d. Colossians 3:13

_____

_____

Personal Application
1. After studying the previous Scriptures, what can you personally say to frustrated people who ask, "Where is God in my family's suffering"?

_____

_____

_____

2. How can the knowledge that the Lord has forgiven you personally of your sins (if you are already a believer) impact your ability to forgive others who hurt you?

_____

_____

2. Blessed Be the Tie that Binds

The Bible has much to say about family relationships. Read the following Scriptures in the *New International Version* (NIV) and fill in the blanks.

a. We should bear with one another in _____ (Ephesians 4:2).

b. We should "put on the new self, created to be like God in true _____ and _____" (Ephesians 4:24).

c. We must "put off _____ and speak _____" [with each other] (Ephesians 4:25).

d. We should be angry, but still not _____ (Ephesians 4:26).

e. We should not give "the _____ a _____" (Ephesians 4:27).

f. "He who has been _____ must _____ no longer" (Ephesians 4:28).

g. "Do not let any _____ talk come out of your mouths, but only what is _____ for _____ others up according to their needs" (Ephesians 4:29).

h. "Get rid of all _____, _____ and _____, _____ and _____, along with every form of _____" (Ephesians 4:31).

i. "Be _____ and _____ to one another, _____ each other, just as in Christ God forgave you" (Ephesians 4:32).

Personal Application

Now look at your own biological and church families. List the family ties that you celebrate in both.

Church Ties	Biological Family Ties
_____	_____
_____	_____
_____	_____
_____	_____
_____	_____

3. Being a Part of the Solution

Read the following verses and write in your own words what God is saying to us about peace and relationships.

a. Psalm 34:14

_____

_____

b. Isaiah 26:3

_____

_____

c. Matthew 5:9

_____

_____

d. John 16:33

_____

_____

_____

e. Romans 12:18

_____

_____

_____

f. Philippians 4:6-7

_____

_____

Personal Application

1. According to your understanding of the previous Scriptures, how can you help bring families within your circle of influence back to basic commitment and spiritual values that have traditionally placed God and the celebration of life at the center of community life?

_____

_____

_____

2. In what ways can you offer to your church family and your biological family the peace that God extends to you?

_____

_____

_____

_____

_____

The Family Ties Commitment Activity

God expects His family to dwell together in peace and unity and be a positive witness for Him. Write a prayer thanking God for all the positive ties that bind your church and also your personal family together. In your prayer, also ask God to assist you with meeting some specific needs of the deficient areas in both families.

_____

_____

_____

_____

_____

_____

_____

_____

_____

Amen.

REPAIRING VS. DISRUPTING

Ezra 1:1-8; 2:1-2, 62-70; 3:1-2, 7, 10-13; Isaiah 40:1-14

"Comfort, comfort my people, says your God. Speak tenderly to Jerusalem, and proclaim to her that her hard service has been completed, that her sin has been paid for, that she has received from the LORD's hand double for all her sins" (Isaiah 40:1-2).

Lesson Focus: God's Family Rebuilds—Hurricanes and other acts of nature can destroy both property and families in a matter of seconds or minutes. After the disaster, it is time to heal and rebuild. So it is with families who have suffered years of disruptions from disagreements, monetary challenges, sicknesses, etc. There comes a time for repairing the breach. In the key verse, Israel had suffered greatly from disobeying God. Therefore, God had chastised Israel by allowing Israel's enemies to take the nation into bondage. Now, God offers His chosen people comfort through the prophet Isaiah.

Words and Phrases You Should Know
In preparation for the lesson, familiarize yourself with the following definitions:
- **New Orleans has a rich history**—The city has a history of celebrations and thriving tourist attractions, a melting pot of people from different ethnic groups, a history of birthing music icons, etc.
- **One's soul is anchored in one's hometown**—Having a love for one's hometown: the people, aura, closeness of the people, family, etc.
- **Incorporating safety nets for the poor and working socio-economic groups**—Building for the rich and prosperous, but allowing some structures and jobs for the working classes and poor
- **In the midst of chaos, still praising God and remaining hopeful**—Looking at the cup half full instead of half empty; seeing and appreciating what you have instead of what you do not have, and recognizing that it is through the goodness of Almighty God that you have survived or you are as well off as you are; having a thankful heart in spite of the difficulties
- **"Can-Do" spirit**—In spite of loss, believing that you can still recover or repair the disruptions
- **"God can make a way out of no way"**—Believing that only God can take nothing and make something out of it; believing that God can take the disasters in our lives and turn them into blessings
- **"Trust in the Lord"**—Having faith in an all-knowing, all-present, and all-powerful God in spite of pain and suffering; believing that God will not leave or forsake you, even in the times of trouble

LIFE APPLICATION DISCUSSION QUESTIONS
State your own personal views in answering the following questions:

1. Is God worthy to be praised, even in the midst of chaos and devastation in our lives? Why? Why not?

_____

_____

2. What are some of the timeless spiritual values that have held African American families together through all kinds of disasters for centuries?

_____

3. How can churches help to heal brokenness in the body of Christ?

_____

_____

4. As believers, we are charged by God to help build His kingdom through witnessing. How can the church carry out this mandate?

_____

_____

BIBLE APPLICATION EXERCISES

1. Repairing Jesus' Family

"With praise and thanksgiving they sang to the LORD: "He is good; his love to Israel endures forever" (Ezra 3:11). As you think on how Jesus' family sometimes needs repairing, review the following verses and then restate their truths in your own words. Ask the Holy Spirit to help you to commit them to your memory.

a. Psalm 106:10

_____

_____

b. Psalm 107:1-2

_____

_____

c. Psalm 108:3-4

_____

_____

d. Psalm 116:1-2

_____

_____

Personal Application

1. What comfort do the promises of God, which are found in His Holy Word, bring you in your own times of mental, physical, or spiritual troubles?

_____

_____

_____

_____

_____

2. How can you share the Good News of salvation with someone who feels hopeless?

_____

_____

_____

_____

_____

2. God Offers Hope for Our Broken Lives

God offers hope for our broken lives first through His salvation by believing on the Lord Jesus Christ. In fact, in Him, we are more than conquerors because God works in everything for our good. He is with us in pain and persecution. Use Romans 8:35-39, NIV, to help you fill in the blanks.

"Who shall separate us from the _____ of Christ? Shall _____ or _____

or _____ or _____ or _____ or _____

or _____? As it is written: 'For your sake we face _____ all the day long; we are

considered as _____ to be _____.' No, in _____ these things we are more than

_____ through him who loved us. For I am convinced that neither _____ nor

_____, neither _____ nor _____, neither the _____ nor the

_____, nor any _____, neither _____ nor _____, nor

anything else in all creation, will be able to _____ us from the _____of God that is

in _____ _____ our Lord."

Personal Application

Now explain in your own words what Romans 8:35-39 means to you personally when you are dealing with the struggles of life.

_____

_____

_____

_____

_____

3. Being a Part of the Solution

Many Hurricane Katrina victims could still praise God in the midst of their suffering because they trusted in God in spite of their circumstances. Read the following verses and write how you can hold on to God in the midst of troubles and know that God is holding on to you.

a. Psalm 23

_____

_____

b. Psalm 91:1-2

_____

_____

c. Psalm 127

_____

_____

d. Isaiah 40:27-29

_____

_____

e. Isaiah 61:1-3

_____

_____

f. Romans 8:1-2

_____

_____

Personal Application

1. Now that you have accepted Jesus Christ as your personal Savior, what repairs has God made in your life?

_____

_____

_____

_____

_____

2. What praises have you offered to God because of what He has done in your life?

_____

_____

_____

_____

_____

The Family Ties Commitment Activity

It is a good thing to be able to celebrate the victories that God has helped us to achieve. Prayerfully consider some of the good things that have happened in your life where you know that God made the difference. Thank God for repairing troubled families (biological and church) and bringing about deliverance when no one else could. Write a prayer of thanksgiving.

_____

_____

_____

_____

_____

_____

_____

_____

Amen.